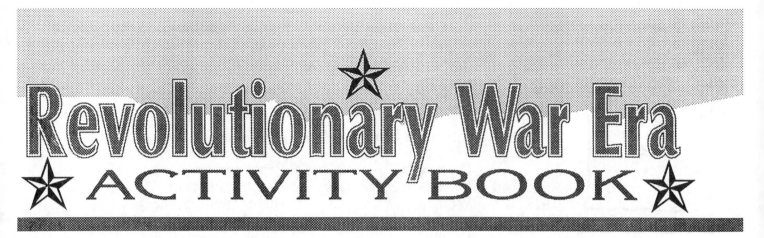

Author	Linda Milliken
Editor	Kathy Rogers
Design	Mary Jo Keller
Illustrator	Barb Lorseyedi

© 1996 **EDUPRESS, INC.** • P.O. Box 883 • Dana Point, CA 92629
www.edupressinc.com
ISBN 1-56472-107-8
Printed in USA

Table of Contents

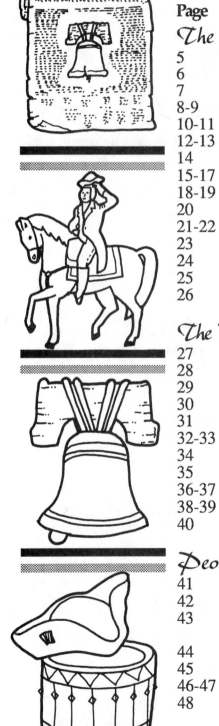

Literature List

• *George the Drummer Boy*
by Nathaniel Benchley;
Harper LB 1977. (1-2)
The story of the beginning of the American
Revolution from the viewpoint of a young
British soldier.

• *The Boston Coffee Party*
by Doreen Rappaport;
Harper LB 1988. (1-3)
Angry women force a greedy merchant to
turn over coffee in this true Revolutionary
War incident.

• *George Washington*
by Ingri & Edgar D'Aulaire;
Doubleday 1936. (2-3)
A simple recounting of the life of the first
president.

• *Sam the Minuteman*
by Nathaniel Benchley;
Harper LB 1969. (2-4)
This book gives information on the way of
life at the beginning of the Revolution.

• *Buttons for General Washington*
by Peter & Connie Roop;
Carolrhoda LB 1986. (2-3)
A 14-year-old boy carries secret messages to
General Washington in the buttons on his
coat. Based on a true story.

• *The American Revolution: War for
   Independence*
by Alden R. Carter;
Watts LB 1992. (3-6)
A summary of the main causes, events, and
battles, with color paintings, maps and
etchings.

• *George Washington: 1st President of the
   United States*
by Lucille Falkof;
Garrett LB 1989. (5-7)
Life story of the first president.

• *The Story of Lexington and Concord*
by R. Conrad Stein;
Childrens LB 1983. (3-6)
A re-creation of two famous battles of the
Revolutionary War.

• *The Story of the Surrender at Yorktown*
by Zachary Kent;
Childrens LB 1989. (3-6)
After a brief history of the Revolution, this
account tells about the last great battle in
Virginia.

• *The Story of Valley Forge*
by R. Conrad Stein;
Childrens LB 1985. (4-6)
An account of the ordeal faced by George
Washington and his men at Valley Forge
during the American Revolution.

• *Our Declaration of Independence*
by Joy Schleifer;
Millbrook LB 1992. (4-6)
An illustrated history of the writing of the
Declaration of Independence and its
significance.

• *The American Revolution: Colonies in
   Revolt*
by Alden R. Carter;
Watts LB 1988. (4-7)
This story of the Revolutionary War begins
in 1760 when King George III is crowned.

• *Concord and Lexington*
by Judie Nordstrom;
Macmillan LB 1993. (4-6)
History and monuments of these two
historic towns, plus their place in the
American Revolution.

• *Why Don't You Get a Horse, Sam
   Adams?*
by Jean Fitz;
Putnam 1974. (3-5)
This story is a humorous re-creation of
Revolutionary times.

Farmer

Historical Aid

During the Revolutionary War era, owning land was the goal of most Americans. Nine out of ten were farmers who made their living from the land and wished to pass the ownership on to their children. Those who owned land were called *freeholders* or *yeomen*.

Farmers' tools were simple and their use required heavy labor. Fields were tilled with wooden plows pulled by oxen. Seeds were sown by hand. At harvest time, crops were cut with a hand-held sickle. On the family farm, women and children were valuable workers.

Project

Make a cardboard sickle and compare it with modern-day tools.

Materials

- Toilet paper tube
- Masking tape
- Cardboard box
- Exacto® blade or heavy-duty scissors
- Pencil

Directions

1. Cut one side off the cardboard box.

2. Use the pencil to trace a large letter "C" on the cardboard. Make one end pointed. Create a two-inch (5 cm) long large notch at the other.

3. Insert the notch into the paper tube. Pinch the end closed around the notch. Secure with masking tape.

Extended Activity

- *Head outside and pretend to mow the lawn or cut down bushes with your sickle. How long might the job take compared to mowing with modern-day tools?*

- *What modern-day tools replace the sickle?*

Craftsmen

Historical Aid

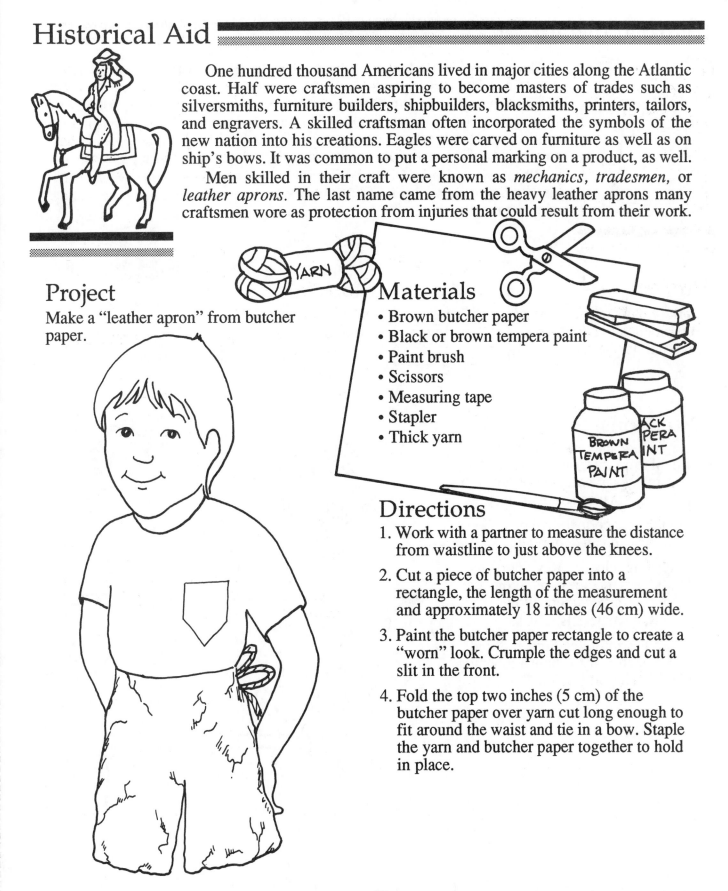

One hundred thousand Americans lived in major cities along the Atlantic coast. Half were craftsmen aspiring to become masters of trades such as silversmiths, furniture builders, shipbuilders, blacksmiths, printers, tailors, and engravers. A skilled craftsman often incorporated the symbols of the new nation into his creations. Eagles were carved on furniture as well as on ship's bows. It was common to put a personal marking on a product, as well.

Men skilled in their craft were known as *mechanics, tradesmen,* or *leather aprons.* The last name came from the heavy leather aprons many craftsmen wore as protection from injuries that could result from their work.

Project

Make a "leather apron" from butcher paper.

Materials
- Brown butcher paper
- Black or brown tempera paint
- Paint brush
- Scissors
- Measuring tape
- Stapler
- Thick yarn

Directions

1. Work with a partner to measure the distance from waistline to just above the knees.

2. Cut a piece of butcher paper into a rectangle, the length of the measurement and approximately 18 inches (46 cm) wide.

3. Paint the butcher paper rectangle to create a "worn" look. Crumple the edges and cut a slit in the front.

4. Fold the top two inches (5 cm) of the butcher paper over yarn cut long enough to fit around the waist and tie in a bow. Staple the yarn and butcher paper together to hold in place.

Masters & Apprentices

Historical Aid

The practice of indenturing boys was common during Revolutionary times. An indentured boy was pledged to learn a craft and remain unmarried. He signed a contract stating this intent and became an *apprentice*, obligated to his *master*, a draftsman skilled in his trade and owning his own business. In exchange for work, the master provided food and lodging, and the promise that his skills would be shared with and taught to his apprentice.

When an apprentice turned twenty-one, he became a *journeyman* and was eligible to earn wages. If he was able to save enough money, he could become a master.

Project

Work in pairs, as *master* and *apprentice*, and complete a Revolutionary-era craft.

Materials

- Revolutionary Craft Cards, following
- Various materials as specified on each card
- Books about Revolutionary-era crafts

Directions

1. Reproduce and cut apart the Revolutionary Craft Cards so that several sets are created. Review the cards and discuss each project.

2. Divide into cooperative pairs, a "master" and an "apprentice."

3. Each pair selects a Revolutionary Craft Card, decides on a project to complete, and gathers all the necessary materials.

4. Share the completed projects and invite each pair to share a few facts about their "profession."

Silversmith

Most towns had a silversmith who made valuable pieces of silver such as candlesticks, medals, and coffee or tea pots.

Use cardboard and aluminum foil to create a platter, tray, bowl or cup.
Use a toothpick to engrave designs in the foil. Engrave the initials of the craftsmen (and women), as well.

Engraver

Before cameras were invented, important events were recreated through the technique of engraving.

Create an "engraving." Brush a thick layer of black tempera paint on white paper.
Use a toothpick to draw a picture in the paint. Create a paper frame for the engraving.

Printer

The printer selected metal type, inked it, then pressed it onto paper to create words and sentences, letter by letter.

Fold a large sheet of construction paper into four sections.
Cut out individual letters from magazines and paste them to the construction paper to create a newspaper.

Carpenter

Master woodworkers constructed buildings and made tables, chairs and other furnishings.

Use building materials to construct a shelf, box, or other woodworking project.
Learn how to sand and finish. (You might even try stenciling a design on the finished project!)

Clockmakers

Clockmakers carved gears from brass and pewter disks. They sold only clockworks and faces. A cabinetmaker made the case.

Combine the skills of a clockmaker and cabinetmaker to make a clock. Use paper and a cereal box to cut, glue and create a clock face with a fancy case.

Ship Builder

Wooden ships were built in every seaport on the Atlantic coast. Shipwrights bolted timbers together and bent planks to create a frame.

Use lumber scraps, craft sticks, toothpicks, nails, and carpentry tools to construct a model ship.
Test your ship in a tub of water. Is it sea worthy?

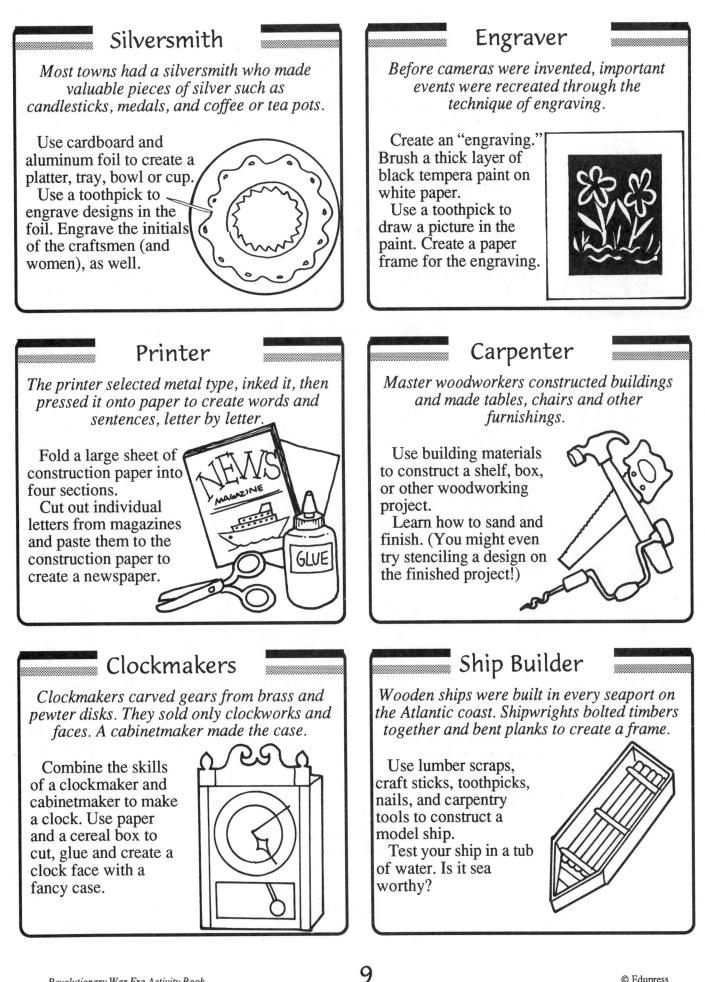

Women

Historical Aid

The life of women during the Revolutionary War era revolved around the home. Girls married at a young age, and as wives and mothers they had many responsibilities. Women spent their days preparing food, tending livestock, supervising farm work, and making the household clothes and linens. Few women had careers. Some women taught children in schools, tended shops or taverns, or worked as seamstresses.

There are stories of women who took part in the Revolutionary War. Margaret Corbin went to war with her husband, and when he was killed in battle, took over the firing of his cannon. Molly Hays became known as Molly Pitcher when she carried water to the soldiers on the battlefield. Deborah Sampson disguised herself as a man and fought as a soldier.

Dairying, or tending to the family cows and their milk products, was a full-time job. One chore that was often shared by women and children was butter-making. Cream was poured into a wooden or earthenware keg, called a *churn.* The keg was fitted with a tight lid in which there was a hole. A paddle, or *dasher*, went through the hole. As the dasher was pushed up and down, butterfat was removed from the milk, eventually forming a lump of butter.

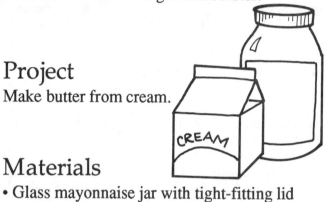

Project
Make butter from cream.

Materials
• Glass mayonnaise jar with tight-fitting lid
• 1 pint (473 ml) cream, well chilled

Directions
1. Pour cream into mayonnaise jar and close securely.

2. Take turns shaking the jar vigorously. It will take 15 to 20 minutes before butter starts to form.

3. Pour off liquid. Serve butter on bread or crackers.

Women

A woman in the Revolutionary era carried her belongings around in a *pocket*, a cloth bag tied around her waist, usually under her skirt. Pockets could be very plain or very ornate. Some were made of patchwork or were decorated with beautiful embroidery. A pocket might contain keys, sewing thread, pins, needles, a baby's bib, or a Bible.

Project

Design a pocket and fill it with objects used by a Revolutionary War-era woman.

Materials

- Two pieces fabric, 8 x 12 inches (20 x 30 cm)
- Needle, thread
- Ribbon or yarn
- Scissors
- Household items

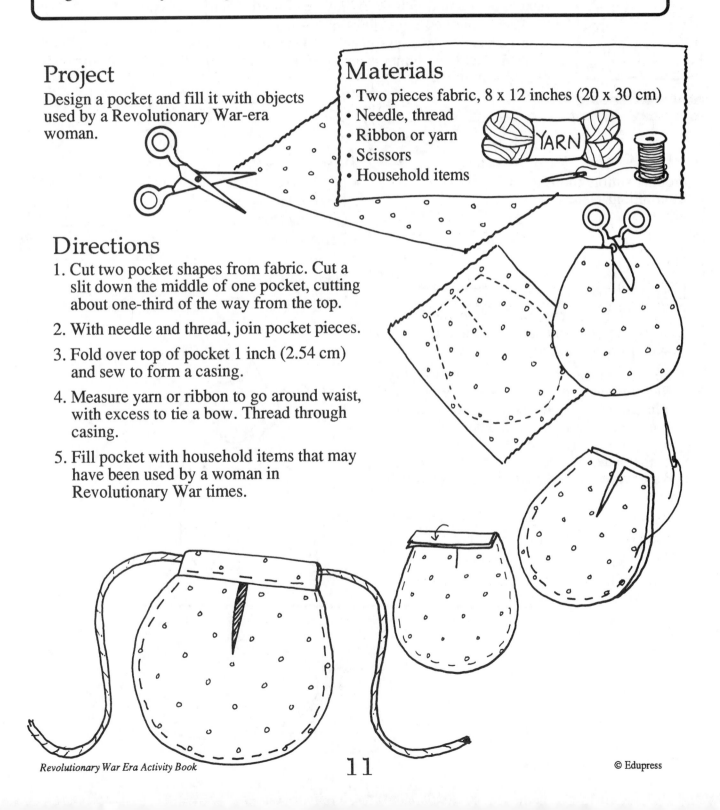

Directions

1. Cut two pocket shapes from fabric. Cut a slit down the middle of one pocket, cutting about one-third of the way from the top.

2. With needle and thread, join pocket pieces.

3. Fold over top of pocket 1 inch (2.54 cm) and sew to form a casing.

4. Measure yarn or ribbon to go around waist, with excess to tie a bow. Thread through casing.

5. Fill pocket with household items that may have been used by a woman in Revolutionary War times.

Food and Cooking

Historical Aid

The kitchen fireplace was used for all cooking tasks. An iron pot hung from a crane. Frying was done in a long-handled iron skillet that stood high on three legs. Roasting was done on a spit inside a sheet-iron box with one open side facing the fire. Baking was done in a fireplace built in the wall, next to the main fireplace. A stove was used strictly for heating.

People ate large quantities of animal fat, and few green vegetables and fruits. Diseases such as scurvy, rickets, and cholera were common. Food spoiled quickly without means for storing it properly. Frozen ice from ponds provided minimal cooling.

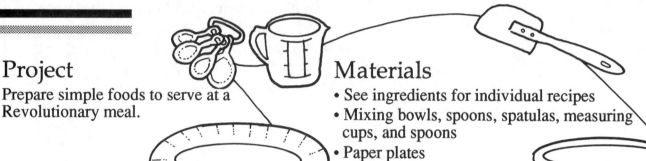

Project

Prepare simple foods to serve at a Revolutionary meal.

Materials

- See ingredients for individual recipes
- Mixing bowls, spoons, spatulas, measuring cups, and spoons
- Paper plates
- Plastic forks and knives
- White butcher paper

Directions

1. Review the recipes. Divide into cooperative groups to plan and carry out the tasks of food and table preparation.

2. Serve the meal as if you were in a wealthy Revolutionary-era home. Set the table with a white butcher paper "cloth" and a plate for everyone. Lay a fork on the table, tines down, to the left of the plate. Set a knife to the right of the plate. (No napkins were used; mouths were wiped with the edge of the tablecloth!)

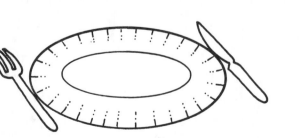

Cider

Most adult men started the day with a "draft" of hard cider, beer, or whiskey and water. Other beverages were tea and coffee.

Directions:

1. Heat **water** in a pan on a hot plate. Place several **tea bags** in the hot water to brew tea. Ladle the hot tea into Styrofoam™ or heat-sensitive cups.
2. Offer an alternate drink: cold **apple cider**.

Cornbread

Bread was served at most meals. Butter was often sliced and eaten like cheese. The poor put molasses on bread instead of butter.

Directions:

1. Make **cornbread** according to package directions.
2. Serve with **butter** slices and small cups of **molasses** for experimental "dipping."

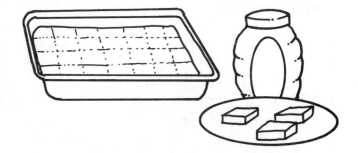

Blood Pudding

The city's less fortunate had especially poor diets. Their meat, called blood pudding, *consisted of beef and pig blood cooked with meat scraps and stuffed into sausage skins. With it they ate bread and molasses. A prosperous family would dine on eight or ten food items, including boiled goose and roasted turkey.*

Directions:

1. Cut **sausage** into slices.
2. Lightly fry in an electric skillet.
3. Spoon into a large bowl for serving.

Dining

Historical Aid

A formal dinner in a wealthy home lasted three or four hours. Plates were porcelain, spoons were silver, elegant rounded knives and three-tined forks were steel with silver or bone handles. A dinner plate stayed on a warming rack until needed. When forks were introduced, napkins were eliminated; guests wiped their mouth with the tablecloth. Sometimes finger bowls were used. Many well-mannered people used the blade of the knife for transferring food from plate to mouth.

Simpler homes owned blue-printed pottery, or cream-colored Wedgwood™. Plates with "American scenes" on them also became popular.

Project

Paint a dinner plate with an American scene.

Materials

- Paper plates
- Pencils
- Watercolor paint and brushes

Directions

1. Brainstorm a list of images that remind students of a typical "American scene." For example: children in a classroom; parents at a soccer field.

2. Choose a scene from the list and sketch it on a paper plate.

3. Use watercolor paints to complete the sketch. Add an edge of bright green or blue paint.

4. Display the plates in a bulletin board.

Clothing

Historical Aid

Clothing of the Revolutionary era was generally made of linen, wool, or a combination of these, called linsey-woolsey. Work clothes and clothing worn by farmers included loose-fitting smocks and loose breeches for men, loose dresses with elbow-length sleeves for women. Clothing for wear in the city or for church was more stylish.

Children dressed in the same styles as adults, with the exception of very young children, who wore long smocks or aprons.

Men

Men of the Revolutionary era wore skirted coats, and tricorn (three-cornered) hats. With these, they wore long stockings and leather shoes decorated with metal buckles. They sometimes wore white-powdered wigs, although by 1776 many men preferred to powder their own hair white, instead.

Women

Women wore dresses with long, bell-shaped skirts. The sleeves were elbow-length, and were sometimes trimmed with linen ruffles. Over their shoulders they often wore a triangular piece of fabric called a *kerchief*. They also wore buckled shoes, and for everyday often wore a cap. For very formal wear, women might also wear a powdered wig or powder their hair.

Clothing

Project
Recreate the clothing styles of Revolutionary-era men and women.

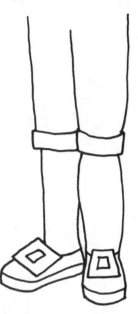

Girls

1. Borrow long, full skirts and aprons from parents.

2. Fold a 36-inch (1 m) square of fabric in half diagonally. Wrap around shoulders, securing with a safety pin in front.

3. Cover two 2-inch (5 cm) squares of cardboard with aluminum foil and attach to shoes.

4. Follow directions to make cap.

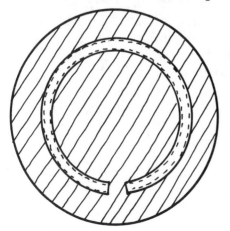

Boys

1. Roll long pant legs up to just below knee and secure with a rubber band.

2. Wear long sports socks and secure under edges of pant legs.

3. Cover two 2-inch (5 cm) squares of cardboard with aluminum foil and attach to shoes.

4. Follow directions (following page) to make three-corner hat.

Cap

1. Cut a circle from a 24-inch (61 cm) square of fabric.

2. Sew a casing of seam binding two inches (5 cm) from the edge of circle.

3. Measure elastic to fit child's head plus one inch (2.54 cm).

4. Run elastic through casing and secure.

Three-Cornered Hat

Directions

1. Trace pattern onto three pieces of **black construction paper** and cut out.

2. **Staple** ends of pieces together in a triangular shape, sizing to fit head.

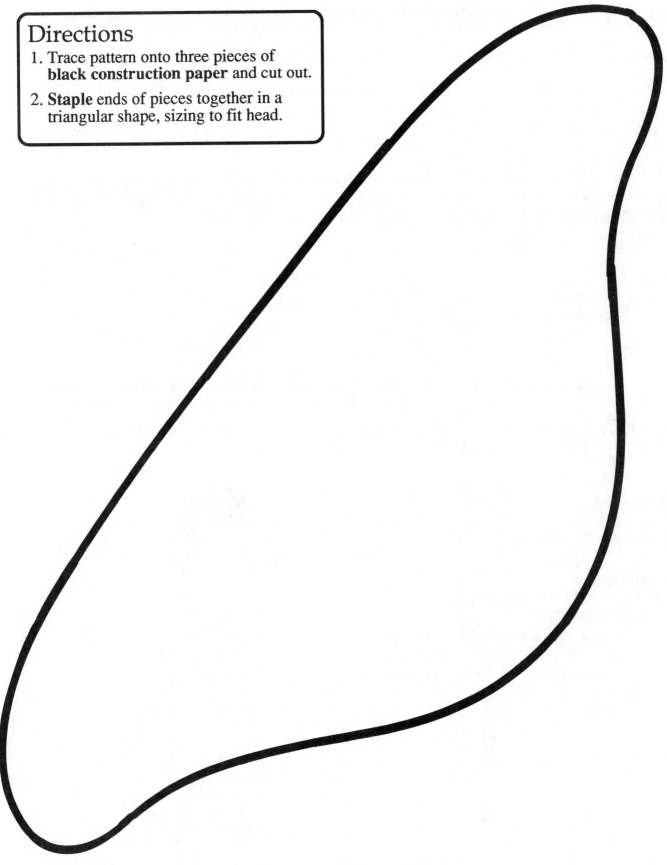

Children

Historical Aid

At the time of the Revolutionary War, almost one half of all Americans were under sixteen years of age. There were many large families in spite of the fact that many children never survived childhood because of disease, poor diets, and inadequate medical care. The average family had ten to twelve children. All were needed to help on the farm. Most children who went to school, walking as much as three miles each way, learned to read, write, and "do sums."

It was a new American idea for a man to divide his estate among all his children rather than passing it on to his eldest son. Marriages for girls, as early as fifteen years of age, were the general rule.

Project

Create an item that a Revolutionary child might have owned.

Materials

• See individual projects

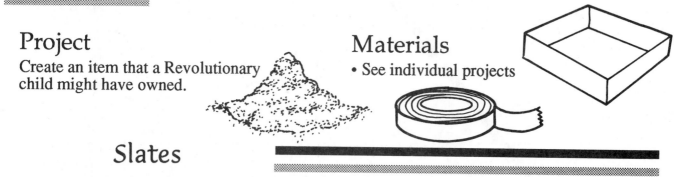

Slates

Children practiced writing and sums on small slates. If a slate was not available, the children spread sand on boards and wrote in it with their fingertips.

Materials:
• Gift box lid
• Sand or loose dirt
• Masking tape

Directions:
1. Tape the corners of the box lid to strengthen them.
2. Pour about one-quarter inch (.6 cm) of sand in the lid.
3. Conduct a spelling or math lesson using the "sand-slates" for responses.

Porringer

A porringer, *a small bowl usually crafted from pewter, was often given as a gift to a child at birth. Well-to-do families presented porringers crafted from silver. American-made porringers featured a carved handle similar to the shape of a crown.*

Materials:
- Paper bowl
- Aluminium foil
- Lightweight cardboard
- Scissors   • Tape

Directions:

1. Cut a handle shape as shown from the cardboard. Cut a slot in the bowl and insert the handle into the slot. Use tape to hold the handle in place.

2. Cover the bowl and handle with aluminum foil.

Wooden Doll

Children played with toys made from simple materials. While some dolls were made from leather, most were created with wood. A "penny wooden" doll was distinguished by its wooden joints and a peg on top of its head.

Materials:
- Old-fashioned wooden clothespin
- Fabric scraps
- Thin-tipped marking pens
- Scissors   • Needle, thread
- Rubber bands   • Glue   • Yarn

Directions:

1. Use marking pens to draw a face on the clothespin head.

2. Fashion clothing from the fabric scraps. Sew with needle and thread, or glue fabric pieces together.

3. Dress the doll in the clothes. A rubber band may hold the clothing in place.

4. Add yarn hair.

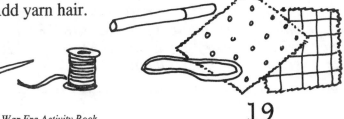

Education

Historical Aid

Children did not have to go to school during the Revolutionary era. That decision was made by the parents, who had to pay for education. Many wanted their children to read so they could study the Bible, often the only book a family owned. Ordinary people and poor families did not have money to pay for a teacher. More importantly, their children were needed to help with the work. Country families would often hire one tutor for the entire community.

City boys took up a trade and became apprentices or master craftsmen. Wealthy families sent their sons to college. Girls learned the skills required for motherhood and home management.

Project

Make a book cover similar to those used by Revolutionary-era school children.

Materials

- Brown paper bag (thin vinyl may be substituted for the paper bag)
- Clear tape or masking tape
- Double-stick Velcro®
- Scissors   • Ruler   • Pencil

Directions

1. Cut the paper bag open and lay it flat.

2. Choose a book to cover. Open the book and lay it on top of the paper bag. Mark the bag with a line along the top and bottom edges of the book. Measure four inches (10 cm) from the edges of the book. Cut along the lines to create a rectangle.

3. Fold one end in at the four-inch (10 cm) mark and tape the top and bottom closed. Cut the other end to create a tab, as shown.

4. Slide the book jacket into the folded end. Wrap the tab end over the closed book. Place a small piece of double-stick Velcro® on the tab and book cover where they meet.

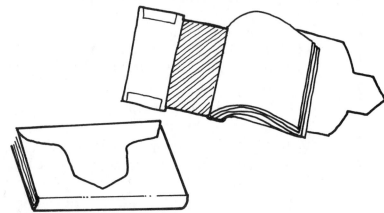

Extended Activity

- *Noah Webster wrote the first American speller in 1783. The cost? Fourteen cents. The speller was popular for more than a hundred years and sold more than 100 million copies. Webster also wrote a grammar book and a dictionary. Look in your home and classroom libraries to see if you have a modern version of Webster's dictionary.*

Sampler

Historical Aid

Needlework was important to Revolutionary-era women in cities and on farms. As soon as a young girl was able to hold a needle, she began working on her sewing skills. One way she did this was with a *sampler*, a small square or strip of cloth covered with different needlework patterns.

Letters, numerals, quotations, and verses were stitched into the sampler. Sometimes a girl would add her name, age, and the date the sampler was made. Samplers eventually became part of a girl's formal instruction and became evidence of educational accomplishments. Many styles and shapes of samplers were produced in the United States until the end of the 1800s.

Project

Create a mock cross-stitch sampler on graph paper.

Materials

- Graph paper, following
- Lightweight white paper
- Colored pencils
- Half-sheet colored construction paper
- Glue

Directions

1. Reproduce the graph paper on lightweight white paper.

2. Simulate a cross-stitch by making an "X" in each square with a colored pencil. Place the "stitches" on the graph paper to spell out the alphabet, or personal information.

3. Display the sampler by mounting it on a colored construction paper frame.

Graph Paper

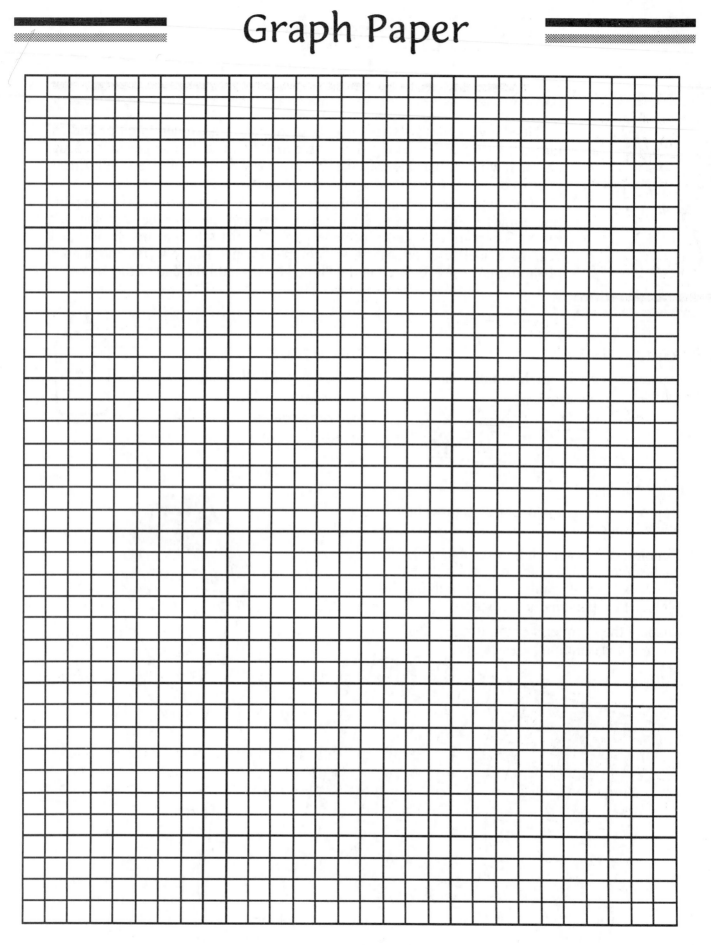

Postal Service

Historical Aid

The United States established a postal system in 1782. Mail was packed in coarse bags made from a heavy woven material. The bags were carried by stagecoaches that had established regular lines from city to city, advertising their routes in the newspapers. Mail for small villages with no post office was left at a store or an inn. No stamps existed. An addressee usually paid the postage when he received the letter. Distance, not weight, determined the postage. There were no envelopes or postcards. The letter was folded twice and twice again and held with a blob of sealing wax. Sometimes an engraved seal was stamped into the wax.

Project

Establish a Revolutionary-era postal system in the classroom.

Materials

- Burlap
- Thick yarn
- Stickers
- Large needle
- Plain writing paper
- Poker chips or other "coins"

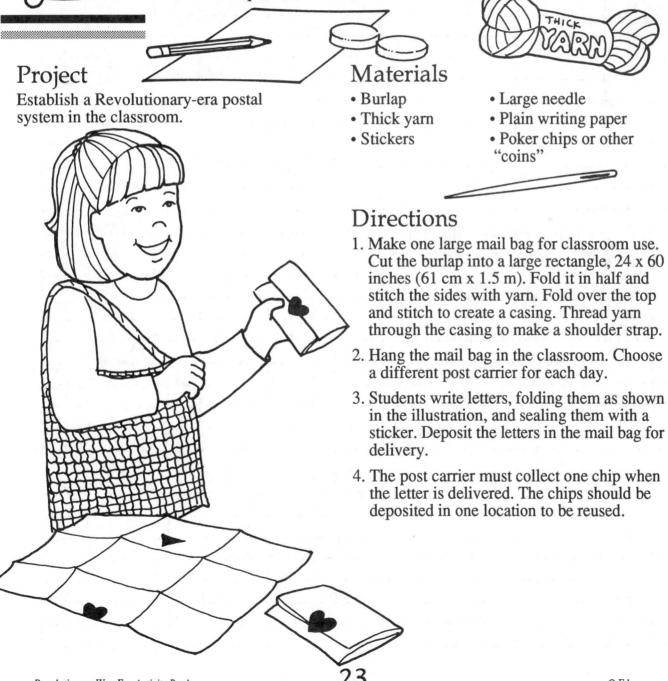

Directions

1. Make one large mail bag for classroom use. Cut the burlap into a large rectangle, 24 x 60 inches (61 cm x 1.5 m). Fold it in half and stitch the sides with yarn. Fold over the top and stitch to create a casing. Thread yarn through the casing to make a shoulder strap.

2. Hang the mail bag in the classroom. Choose a different post carrier for each day.

3. Students write letters, folding them as shown in the illustration, and sealing them with a sticker. Deposit the letters in the mail bag for delivery.

4. The post carrier must collect one chip when the letter is delivered. The chips should be deposited in one location to be reused.

Handbills

Historical Aid

The primary way that political opinion and news about events could be spread was through the printed word. Forty-four newspapers were published in the colonies in 1775. Most were four-page, tabloid-size papers that were published weekly. The average circulation was five hundred copies. By 1790 there were 90 newspapers in the country, and by 1810 there were almost 240.

A *handbill*, or *broadside*, was a single page that a printer could quickly reproduce to be posted on trees or tavern doors to report the latest news from Europe, or to encourage people to come to a meeting. A handbill was often done in cartoon style, expressing dissatisfaction with government policies.

Project

Create a handbill to post at school.

Materials

- Sheet of plain writing paper
- Black marking pens
- Photocopy machine
- Masking tape

Directions

1. Create a black and white, one page handbill that announces an important school or community event.

2. Add pictures and create text that draws attention to the handbill.

3. Make two photocopies of each handbill.

4. Tape the handbills around school for students to share and read. Don't forget to take them down after a few days!

Extended Activity

- *Look through newspapers for editorial cartoons. Create a current events board featuring the newspaper clippings.*

Flatboat

Historical Aid

In the late 1700s, transporting people and cargo by river on flat-bottomed barges, called flatboats, proved to be the cheapest and easiest way to travel.

Flatboats were built from long planks. They measured up to 50 feet (15.2 m) long and about 15 feet (4.6 m) wide. Their narrow width enabled them to travel the channels of the Ohio and Mississippi Rivers. One end of the flatboat had a sheltered area for sleeping and eating. Some had fences around the sides for protection. Because they drifted with the current, guided by long poles, flatboats could only travel one way. They were taken apart at the end of the trip and the lumber was used for other purposes, often to build homes for the passengers.

Project

Construct a replica of a flatboat.

Directions

1. Cut open one side of the gift box.

2. Paint the craft sticks and gift box. Invert the shoe box lid so that the top becomes the bottom of the flatboat. Paint the sides of the lid.

3. When the paint has dried, glue craft sticks to cover the inside of the lid, breaking the sticks to fit.

4. Glue the gift box to one end of the "flatboat." If you can find two long twigs, tape them to the top of the gift box, as shown in the illustration.

Materials

- Small gift box (approximately 3 inches/ 7.6 cm square)
- Shoe box lid
- Paint brush
- Glue
- Brown tempera paint
- Scissors
- Craft sticks
- Optional: two long twigs, masking tape

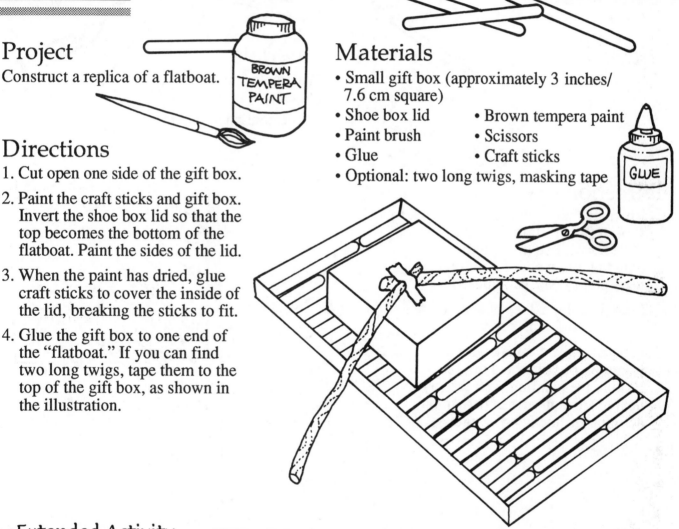

Extended Activity

- *Brainstorm a list of uses for the lumber made available when a flatboat was torn apart. What goods and services might Revolutionary travelers have needed in their new homes?*

- *Conduct experiments involving currents. How can you make an object move against the flow of water?*

Tree of Liberty

Historical Aid

In 1765, the people of Boston designated a giant elm on the main road into town as their Tree of Liberty, where demonstrations opposing British rule and policies were held. Other colonists followed this example and set aside a Tree of Liberty, or erected a giant Liberty Pole, in their towns to serve as a central meeting place where grievances could be expressed.

The image of the Tree of Liberty began appearing all over the colonies, on posters, engravings, and soldier's equipment. It became the most common colonial symbol of the American Revolution.

Project

Paint a Tree of Liberty.

Materials

- Watercolor paints
- Crayons
- White construction paper

Directions

1. Recreate the picture of the Tree of Liberty, as illustrated, on the chalkboard. Use the chalkboard drawing as a model for individual watercolor resist paintings.

2. Heavily color a Tree of Liberty on white construction paper.

3. Paint over the drawing with a watercolor wash of red or blue. Feature the paintings in a display next to student-written paragraphs defining the meaning of liberty.

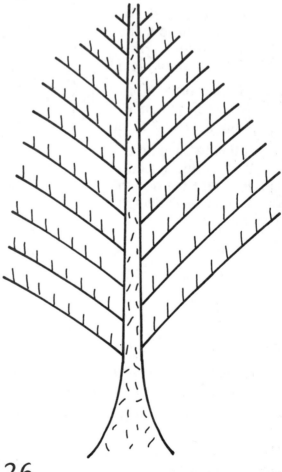

Choosing a Militia

Historical Aid

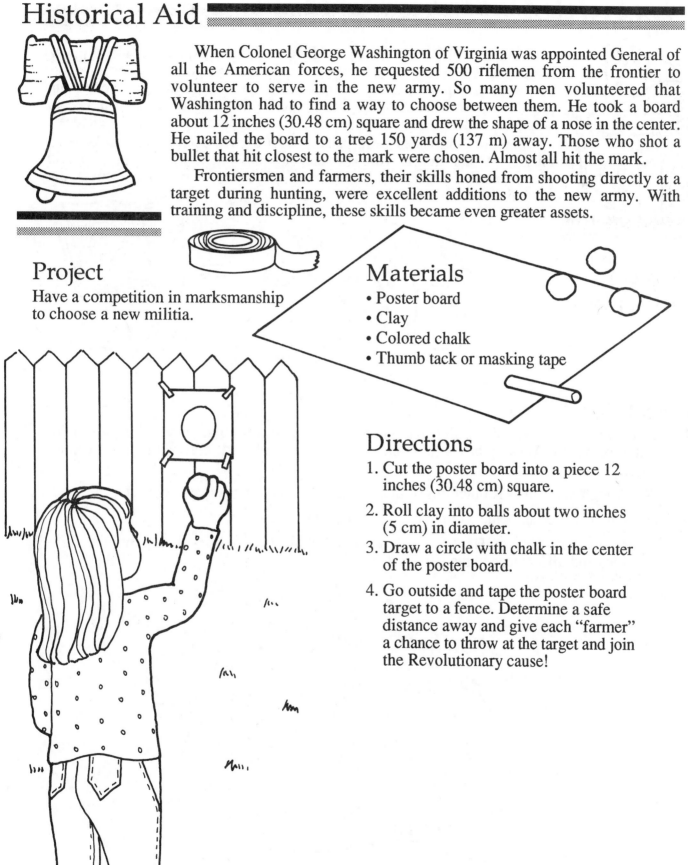

When Colonel George Washington of Virginia was appointed General of all the American forces, he requested 500 riflemen from the frontier to volunteer to serve in the new army. So many men volunteered that Washington had to find a way to choose between them. He took a board about 12 inches (30.48 cm) square and drew the shape of a nose in the center. He nailed the board to a tree 150 yards (137 m) away. Those who shot a bullet that hit closest to the mark were chosen. Almost all hit the mark.

Frontiersmen and farmers, their skills honed from shooting directly at a target during hunting, were excellent additions to the new army. With training and discipline, these skills became even greater assets.

Project

Have a competition in marksmanship to choose a new militia.

Materials

- Poster board
- Clay
- Colored chalk
- Thumb tack or masking tape

Directions

1. Cut the poster board into a piece 12 inches (30.48 cm) square.

2. Roll clay into balls about two inches (5 cm) in diameter.

3. Draw a circle with chalk in the center of the poster board.

4. Go outside and tape the poster board target to a fence. Determine a safe distance away and give each "farmer" a chance to throw at the target and join the Revolutionary cause!

Seamen

Historical Aid

Congress built a small navy of fifty to sixty ships, commanded by local sea captains who recruited crews from their home ports. Americans at sea concentrated on defending American shores, harassing the enemy, and plundering British merchant ships. The British also dispatched a fleet of ships whose job it was to patrol American coastlines and set up blockades.

Ships on both sides were packed with barrels containing lead balls for muskets. Other barrels were on board to hold water, wine, rum, and grain. Many seamen brought with them a keepsake, some small object that reminded them of home.

Project

Create a keepsake collage.

Materials

- Magazines
- Glue
- Scissors
- Construction paper

Directions

1. Imagine that you are boarding a ship that will take you out to sea to fight a war from which you might never return. What things would you want to have "on board" that would most remind you of home?

2. Look through magazines for pictures of these things—special foods, pets, toys, etc.

3. Cut out the pictures and glue them in a collage on construction paper.

4. Assemble the individual collages in one large mural on the classroom wall. Discuss the similarities and differences in the items selected.

28

Feeding the Army

Historical Aid

George Washington estimated that he would need one hundred thousand barrels of flour and twenty million pounds (453.59 metric tons) of meat to feed fifteen thousand soldiers for one year. That quota was never met. The army often went hungry.

It was usually women or children who cooked for the soldiers. When battles were fought near their homes, they fed and cared for the wounded. Some women followed the army, acting as cooks and laundresses. One of the staples was biscuits, called *hardtack*, a mixture of only two ingredients—flour and water. It was tasteless, but had a long shelf life.

Project

Bake a batch of *hardtack*—biscuits served to Revolutionary armies.

Materials

• Flour
• Small mixing bowl for each student
• Waxed paper
• Plastic glass or round cookie cutter
• Plastic fork
• Oven

Directions

1. Add enough water to ¼ cup (59 ml) flour to make a soft, but not sticky, dough.

2. Punch and work the dough for about ten minutes, until the dough is elastic in texture.

3. Roll the dough on a sheet of wax paper to ½-inch (1.27 cm) thickness.

4. Use a plastic glass or circle-shaped cookie cutter to cut the dough into biscuits. Prick each one with a fork.

5. Bake at 450° F (232° C) for about 7 minutes. Turn the oven down to 350° F (177° C) and bake 7 to 10 minutes more. The biscuits should be hard, like a rock. Try to enjoy! Imagine a diet of hardtack!

Canteen

Historical Aid

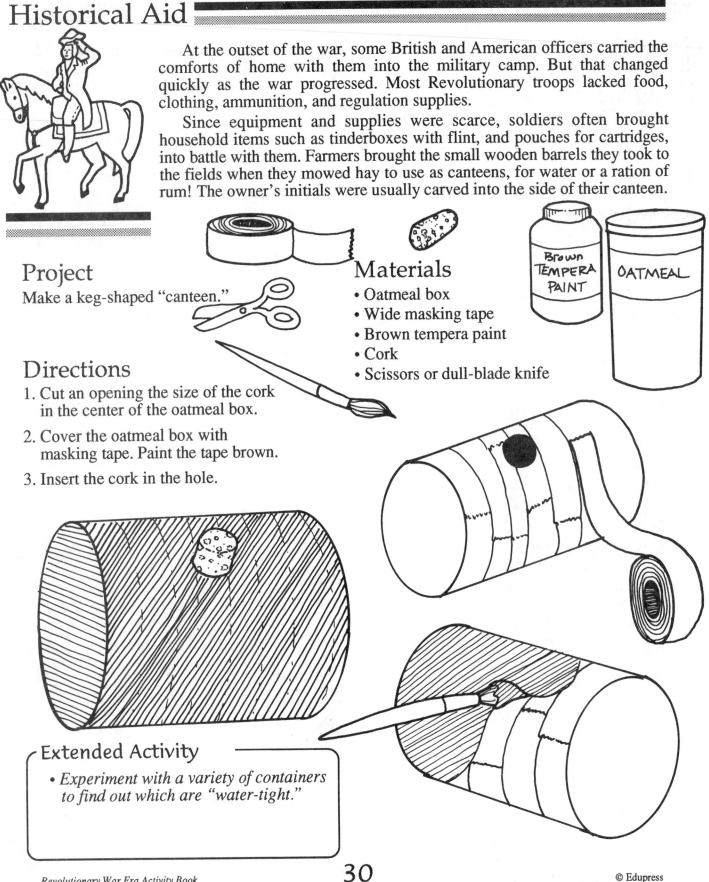

At the outset of the war, some British and American officers carried the comforts of home with them into the military camp. But that changed quickly as the war progressed. Most Revolutionary troops lacked food, clothing, ammunition, and regulation supplies.

Since equipment and supplies were scarce, soldiers often brought household items such as tinderboxes with flint, and pouches for cartridges, into battle with them. Farmers brought the small wooden barrels they took to the fields when they mowed hay to use as canteens, for water or a ration of rum! The owner's initials were usually carved into the side of their canteen.

Project
Make a keg-shaped "canteen."

Materials
- Oatmeal box
- Wide masking tape
- Brown tempera paint
- Cork
- Scissors or dull-blade knife

Directions
1. Cut an opening the size of the cork in the center of the oatmeal box.

2. Cover the oatmeal box with masking tape. Paint the tape brown.

3. Insert the cork in the hole.

Extended Activity
- *Experiment with a variety of containers to find out which are "water-tight."*

Uniforms

Historical Aid

The British soldiers occupying American colonies were nicknamed *redcoats* because of their distinctive bright uniforms. The uniforms of the colonists were almost identical in style, but were bright blue. In addition to uniform coats, soldiers wore light-colored breeches, boots, and tall hats.

In fact, many of the American fighters were dressed in makeshift uniforms, providing their own loose hunting shirts or homemade uniforms. Before the start of the war, George Washington, working as a surveyor in Indian lands, noticed that bright uniforms made soldiers very good targets—they were very easy to spot against the green of hillsides and forests. The everyday clothes of the militiamen made it much easier for them to defend their lands from behind trees and from other hidden positions.

Project

Create a bulletin board showing different styles of uniforms.

Materials

- Book with illustrations of Revolutionary War uniforms, American and British
- Drawing paper
- Markers or crayons
- Brown and green construction paper
- Scissors

Directions

1. After reviewing illustrations, select and draw a soldier in uniform—redcoat, American regular (blue), or militia.

2. Use brown and green construction paper to create a forest of trees on bulletin board.

3. Select a hiding place on the bulletin board for your soldier and pin it in place. Which uniforms are the easiest to hide among the trees?

© Edupress

Baldric & Sword Knot

Historical Aid

The uniforms of both British and American officers could be very elaborate. Coats might be embellished with braid and epaulettes, or shoulder ornaments. Hats sometimes had feathers or *cockades*, which were decorative knots or rosettes made of ribbon.

A soldier's sword was a very important part of his uniform. The sword was carried in a leather shoulder strap called a *baldric*. Swords were sometimes decorated with a *sword knot*, a decorative tassel that was tied to the sword's hilt, or handle.

Project

Make an officer's coat and embellish with sword, baldric and sword knot.

Materials

• See individual projects

Uniform Coat

Materials:
• Paper grocery bag
• Scissors
• Red and blue tempera paint
• Paint brush
• Gold braid trim
• Glue

Directions:
1. Cut up the front center of bag. Cut neck and arm openings, as illustrated.
2. Paint bag red or blue.
3. Glue gold braid around front and neck openings to decorate.

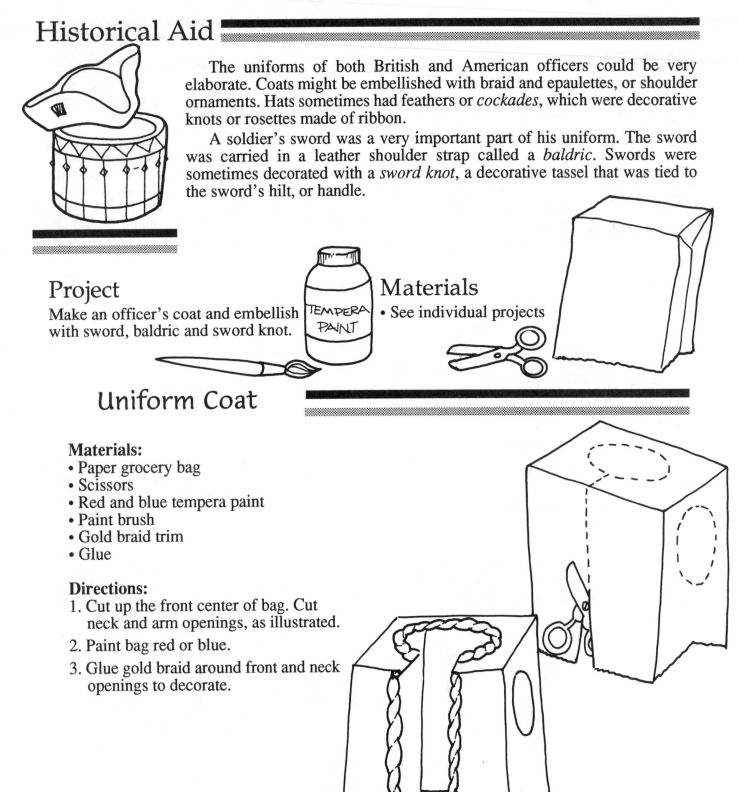

Sword

Swords could be very interesting and individual in design. The hilt, *or handle might be very ornate, decorated with engraving.*

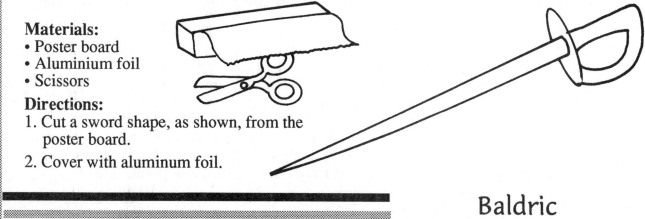

Materials:
• Poster board
• Aluminium foil
• Scissors

Directions:
1. Cut a sword shape, as shown, from the poster board.
2. Cover with aluminum foil.

Baldric

The baldric was a leather holder that supported a sword at the wearer's side. It draped over the shoulder or across the chest, letting the hilt of the sword hang just below waist-level.

Materials:
• Strip of brown felt, 3 inches (7.5 cm) wide and long enough to loop over shoulder
• Brown felt rectangle, approximately 2½ inches x 8½ inches (8.5 cm x 21.5 cm)
• Stapler

Directions:
1. Fold felt rectangle into a tube, being sure it fits around sword blade. Staple together.
2. Fit felt strip across torso and adjust to size. Staple to form loop.
3. Staple holder to strap just below waist level.

Sword Knot

A sword knot was a decorative tassel that attached to the sword handle.

Materials:
• Yarn in a variety of colors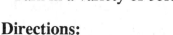

Directions:
1. Cut several strands of yarn in lengths of 18 inches (48 cm). Tie together at one end.
2. Braid yarn and secure at other end.
3. Make two tassels of yarn and tie to either end of braid.
4. Tie completed sword knot around handle of sword.

Fife and Drum

Historical Aid

The British made up the song "Yankee Doodle" to insult the Americans. They said a "Yankee Doodle" was a backwoods hick who didn't know how to fight. When the British marched to Lexington and Concord, they wore their red dress uniforms, and their drummers and pipers played "Yankee Doodle." After winning that battle, the Americans sang the song with pride. It became the most popular song of the American Revolution.

Fife (an instrument similar to a flute) and drums provided rousing music as well as signals on battlefields. Women expressed their support for the Revolution by singing patriotic songs at ceremonial functions.

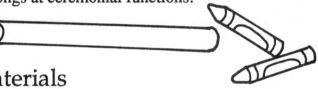

Project

Make a fife and drums. Invite those who play flutes to join in with drummers and practice a military march to the tune, "Yankee Doodle."

Materials

- Large coffee can
- Construction paper
- Paper towel tube
- Record or tape player
- Tape or record of song "Yankee Doodle"
- Yarn
- Masking tape
- Crayons
- Scissors

Directions

Fife

1. Cut six holes in the top of a paper towel tube.

2. Wrap the tube ends with masking tape.

Drum

1. Measure construction paper the width of the coffee can. Cut a piece long enough to wrap around the can and cover it.

2. Color a patriotic symbol such as an eagle on the paper. Wrap the can and tape the paper in place.

3. Tape yarn, top to bottom, around the coffee can to create a zig-zag effect. Replace the lid on the coffee can.

Powder Horn

Historical Aid

Along with his gun, a militiaman carried a cartridge pouch and a cow or ox horn in which he carried gunpowder. The powder horn was often the same one the soldier carried when hunting before the outbreak of war. On the powder horn he carved designs and pictures which usually included his name, the date and place it was carved, and a slogan reflecting the ideals of freedom.

Military records during the Revolution were sketchy, at best. It was often the powder horn, with its personal information, that provided the only way to identify a soldier who died on the battlefield.

Project

Make a paper powder horn.

Materials

- White or tan construction paper
- Thin-tipped black marking pens
- Clear tape

Directions

1. Use a black marking pen to create pictures on the construction paper. Include date, name, and city.

2. Roll the paper to create a cone. Tape to hold in place.

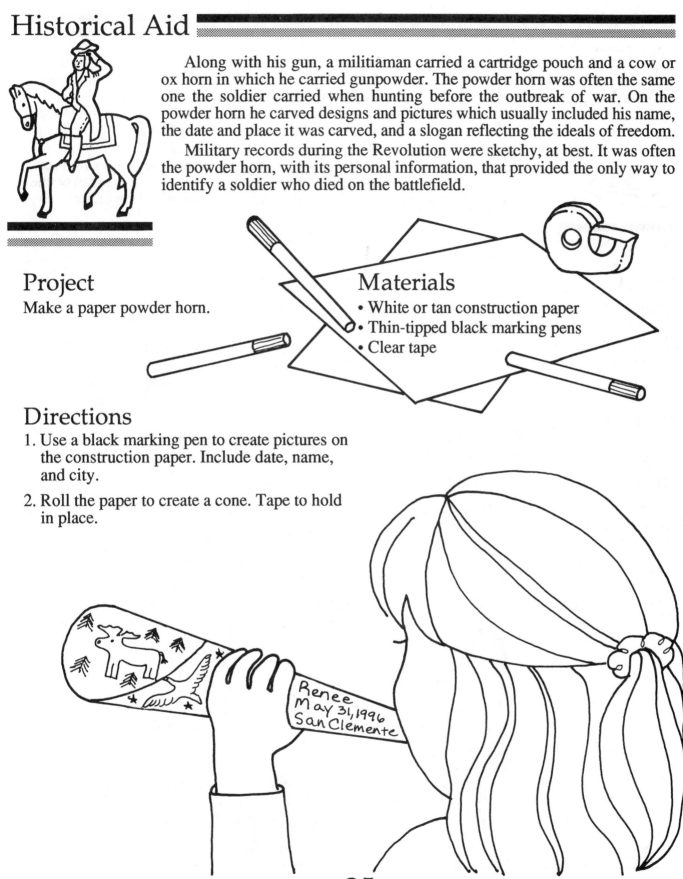

Muskets & Rifles

Historical Aid

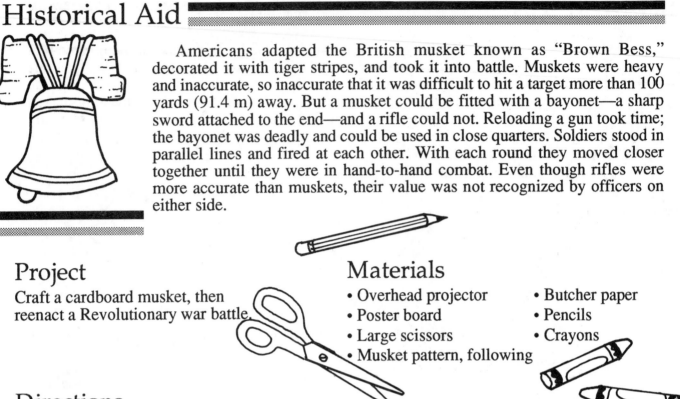

Americans adapted the British musket known as "Brown Bess," decorated it with tiger stripes, and took it into battle. Muskets were heavy and inaccurate, so inaccurate that it was difficult to hit a target more than 100 yards (91.4 m) away. But a musket could be fitted with a bayonet—a sharp sword attached to the end—and a rifle could not. Reloading a gun took time; the bayonet was deadly and could be used in close quarters. Soldiers stood in parallel lines and fired at each other. With each round they moved closer together until they were in hand-to-hand combat. Even though rifles were more accurate than muskets, their value was not recognized by officers on either side.

Project

Craft a cardboard musket, then reenact a Revolutionary war battle.

Materials

- Overhead projector
- Poster board
- Large scissors
- Musket pattern, following
- Butcher paper
- Pencils
- Crayons

Directions

1. Magnify the musket pattern, following, on an overhead projector. The length should be equal to a piece of poster board. Cut several patterns from butcher paper.

2. Trace the pattern on poster board. Cut the musket shape and add tiger stripes.

3. Go outside to stage the reenactment. Divide into two groups. Select a commanding officer for each group. Line up in parallel lines facing each other, at a distance of about 100 yards (91.4 m).

4. One group fires upon command. (One loud noise per soldier, please!) The "enemy" fires once upon command. March ten paces forward and repeat the firing procedure. Continue to march forward until you are in "hand-to-hand" combat range.

Musket Pattern

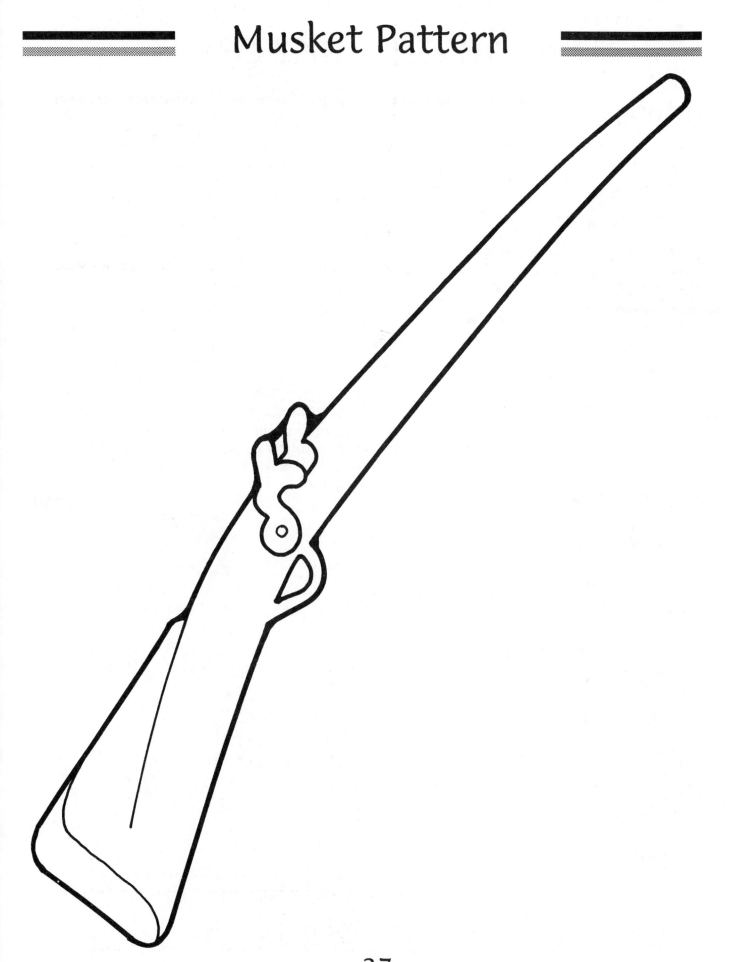

Firing a Cannon

Historical Aid

Six or seven men were needed to fire a Revolutionary cannon. It was a dangerous and noisy task. There was always the chance that the gunpowder would explode inside the cannon barrel, killing all those around it. The life span of a cannoneer was only about six months. Even if he survived, his chances of being deaf were great.

The firing began when the commanding officer shouted, "Worm!" and ended after a sequence of commands with the final shout, "Fire!" The cannon ball exploded out of the gun's mouth at a speed of about 1,000 feet (304.8 m) a second.

Project

Reenact the firing of a Revolutionary cannon.

Materials

• Cannon Firing Reenactment Script, following
• Prop materials:

poster board, shoe box, glue, wire, dish sponge, rubber band, paper towel tubes, flour, paper bag, newspaper, aluminum foil, string, cardboard

Directions

1. Divide into groups of six. Assign roles for the reenactment: Officer, wormer, sponger, loader, rammer, gunner.

2. Make the props:

   Cannon: A poster board tube glued to the top of a shoe box.

   Worm: Wire bent into a corkscrew shape.

   Sponge: A dish sponge fastened with a rubber band to the end of a stick or paper tube.

   Powder: Flour in a paper bag.

   Cannon ball: Large wad of newspaper covered with aluminum foil.

   Ram: Metal clothes hanger, untwisted.

   Fuse: Length of string.

3. Practice the script, then perform the reenactment for an audience.

Reenactment Script

*The **commanding officer** issues each command in a loud voice. As the actions are carried out, the officer reads the script to describe what is happening to the audience.*

1. **"Worm!"**
   The **wormer** twists the worm into the cannon's barrel. This cleans out the barrel and gets it ready for the next round of fire.

2. **"Sponge!"**
   The **sponger** sticks a wet sheepskin into the barrel. That cools it down and puts out sparks left over from previous firings.

3. **"Load!"**
   A **loader** stuffs a bag of gunpowder into the barrel, followed by a big iron ball or grapeshot. Grapeshot is clusters of small iron balls that scatter with great force.

4. **"Ram!"**
   A **rammer**, holding a pole with a wooden disk on its end, pushes the cannon ball or grapeshot and packs the ammunition tightly into the cannon.

5. **"Pick and Prime!"**
   A **gunner** sticks a pick into the barrel and breaks open the ammunition sack. He adds powder in a vent hole and puts a pinch of powder on the ammunition barrel.

6. **"Give!"**
   The **gunner** lights a fuse in preparation for lighting the gunpowder.

7. **"Fire!"**
   The **gunner** uses the fuse to light the powder on top of the barrel. The flame sets off the powder and propels the ball out of the cannon's mouth.

© Edupress

Ammunition

Historical Aid

Patriots made cartridges at home by melting lead and ladling it into molds. There was always a shortage of supplies. British statues were taken down and recycled to make bullets. A half dozen women melted the lead from a statue of King George III of England and turned it into over forty thousand cartridges for use by patriot forces.

American ironworkers made cast-iron cannons and cannon shot. They forged the iron and steel which gunsmiths beat into muskets, bayonets and swords. They also made the necessities for military encampments: ovens and cooking pots, picks, shovels, and spades.

Project

Mold wax to create revolutionary "bullets."

Materials

- Egg carton
- Candles or crayons
- Cooking pan
- Coffee can
- Hot plate or stove
- Ladle
- Hot pads

Directions

1. Fill the pan half-way with water. Set the coffee can inside.

2. Partially fill the coffee can with crayons or candle pieces. (Remove the wicks with tweezers as the wax melts.)

3. When the wax has melted completely, ladle a small amount into egg carton cups.

4. Allow the wax to cool and harden. Peel the egg carton off the hardened wax. Consider the weight of the wax "bullets" compared to iron. With safety in mind, toss the wax "bullet" at a target.

Paul Revere

Historical Aid

Paul Revere was born in Boston, Massachusetts, on January 1, 1735. He was an expert silversmith, and was also well-known for engraving and other types of metal work. After serving for a short time in the militia, he became a courier of information during the Revolutionary War.

Paul Revere is probably best known as one of the riders sent to warn the minutemen of the approach of British troops on the eve of the Battles of Lexington and Concord. On April 18, 1775, British redcoats set out by sea from Boston towards Concord. Patriot organizers hung two lanterns in the steeple of the Old North Church. Paul Revere saw the signal, and along with William Dawes, rode north to alert people in neighboring towns and villages.

Project

Make a paper lantern similar to the lanterns hung in the Old North Church.

Materials

- Half-gallon (1.89 l) milk carton
- Yellow construction paper
- Black construction paper, cut in 1-inch (2.54 cm) strips
- Glue   • Scissors   • Tape

Directions

1. Cut the top off of milk carton to form a rectangular box.

2. Cut yellow construction paper to cover outside of box and tape into place.

3. Place black construction paper strips lengthwise at intervals around the box, being sure that strips of yellow show between the black strips. Glue into place. Trim any excess pieces.

4. Make a handle by gluing each end of a black strip to opposite edges of the top of the box.

5. Glue one black strip around the top edge of the box and a second strip around the bottom.

Boston Tea Party

Historical Aid

On the evening of December 16, 1773, a group of American colonists disguised as Mohawks boarded British ships in Boston harbor and broke open 342 chests of tea, dumping the tea into the water. This "Tea Party" was a violent protest against British taxation in the colonies, and was the first aggressive act taken by the colonists on their quest for independence.

Tea was probably the most popular beverage in the colonies. When the British imposed heavy taxes on tea being imported to the colonies, the colonists rebelled by refusing to drink it. Tea was kept in wooden chests that were often ornate and beautifully decorated.

Project

Make a tea chest and sample different types of tea.

Materials

- Large shoe box with lid
- Brown tempera paint and paint brush
- Scraps of brightly colored construction paper
- Glue
- Spray lacquer
- Several varieties of tea bags

Directions

1. Paint shoe box and lid.

2. Cut designs from construction paper scraps and glue onto box.

3. Spray box with lacquer and let dry.

4. Place tea bags in box. Have a class tea-tasting party.

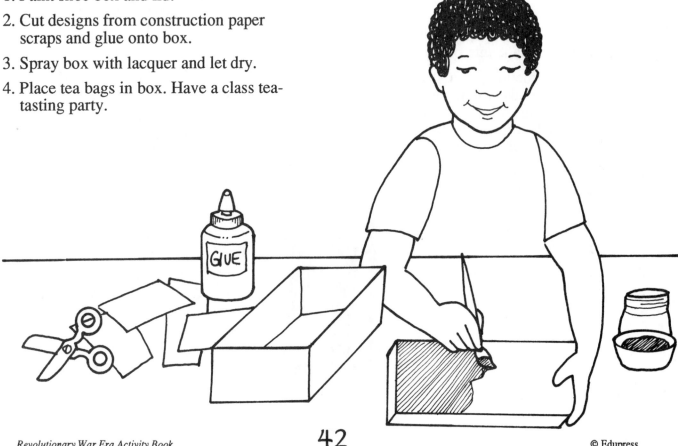

Declaration of Independence

Historical Aid

The Declaration of Independence, written by Thomas Jefferson in about two weeks, is the document in which the American colonies declared their freedom from British rule. The Second Continental Congress, a meeting of delegates from all the colonies, adopted the Declaration on July 4, 1776. On July 19, Congress ordered the Declaration to be *engrossed* (written in beautiful script on parchment). The president of the Congress, John Hancock, was the first to sign. Eventually all 56 members of Congress signed.

The original parchment copy of the Declaration is housed in the National Archives Building in Washington D.C. It is displayed with the United States Constitution and the Bill of Rights.

Project

Create a decorative mural that features each student's signature *engrossed* on a classroom "scroll."

Materials

- Colored marking pens
- Red or blue butcher paper
- White construction paper
- Pencils
- Glue

Directions

1. Create several examples of handwriting with flourishes on the letters on the chalkboard.

2. Each student signs his or her name on a sheet of white construction paper. Use pencil first so that erasures can be made and fancy flourishes can be added.

3. Decorate the signature with colored markers.

4. Glue the signature sheets to the butcher paper. Display on a classroom door or wall.

Minutemen

Historical Aid

In the years before the Revolutionary War, volunteers were organized into military companies and trained to bear arms. These men were called *minutemen* because they were prepared to fight "at a minute's notice."

On April 18, 1775, British Lt. Gen. Thomas Gage ordered his redcoats to destroy the patriots' main supply depot at Concord, Massachusetts. They arrived at Lexington early the next morning. A band of minutemen faced the redcoats on the village green. No one knows who fired the first shot, but eight colonists were killed and ten wounded. Minutemen opposed the advancing British, spurring people from all walks of life to join the cause of liberty.

Project

Play a timed minuteman game.

Materials

- Stopwatch
- Playground
- Whistle
- Paper
- Pencil

Directions

1. Designate two spots on the playground: a starting point and a finishing circle.

2. Divide into two or more groups.

3. Choose one group to go at a time. At a starting signal, the stopwatch is set in motion and the first group races from the starting point to the finishing circle. When everyone in the group is inside the circle, stop the stopwatch and note the time.

4. Repeat the timed activity with the remaining groups. Reward the winning group with a point and repeat the game. The members of the group that finishes with the fastest average time are declared minutemen. Special recess privileges may follow the success!

Native Americans

Historical Aid

There were Native American supporters for both the patriots and the British during the Revolutionary War. Many tribes allied themselves with the redcoats in hopes of stopping the spread of the new nation into their lands. These alliances were often sealed with the giving of valuable gifts such as silver ornaments.

The Oneidas of western New York aided the Americans during the terrible winter at Valley Forge, sending snowshoes to the American soldiers. Both the British and the Americans paid Native Americans for scalps taken from the enemy. A few Native Americans actually became soldiers in one of the opposing armies.

Project

Make an ornamental armlet similar to ornaments given to the Native Americans by the British.

Materials

• Poster board, cut in 3-inch (7.6 cm) strips
• Tape
• Aluminum foil
• Toothpick

Directions

1. Cut poster board strip to fit loosely around upper arm, plus a 1-inch (2.54 cm) overlap.

2. Adjust fit and tape ends of strip together. Cut a scalloped or decorative edge.

3. Cover band with aluminum foil.

4. Use toothpick to trace decorative patterns on the aluminum foil to resemble engraving.

George Washington

Historical Aid

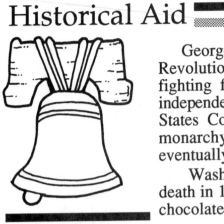

George Washington guided his country for over twenty years during the Revolutionary era and became the chief symbol of what the colonists were fighting for. He commanded the Continental Army that won American independence. He served as president of the convention that wrote the United States Constitution. After the war it was suggested the Army set up a monarchy with Washington as king. He fought against the idea, and eventually became the first man elected President of the United States.

Washington was loved by the people of his time. Especially after his death in 1799, his likeness was used on everything, from cast iron stoves to chocolate candy molds; from statues to paintings.

Project

Complete a project that features the likeness of George Washington.

Materials

- Washington project page, following
- Reference books featuring pictures of Washington
- Colored pencils
- Watercolor paints
- Glue
- Tempera paints
- Small gift boxes
- Cardboard boxes
- Scissors
- Crayons
- Poster board

Directions

1. Set up three areas in the classroom for the completion of each project. Provide the necessary materials at each area. Stock a central table with reference books featuring George Washington.

2. Explain the project choices from the Washington project page.

3. Allow students to go to the project area of choice.

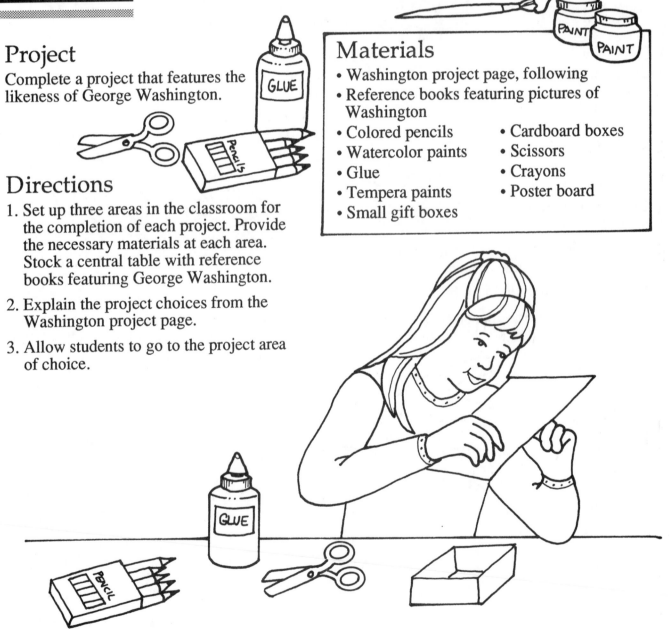

Miniature

Miniatures, *small portraits, appeared on candy boxes, snuff boxes, and pins. George Washington's profile was a popular image for many miniatures.*

Materials:
- Poster board
- Small gift box
- Colored pencils
- Scissors
- Glue

Directions:
1. Cut a small oval from poster board.
2. Sketch and color a profile of Washington's head on the oval to create a miniature.
3. Glue the miniature to the lid of the gift box.

Statue

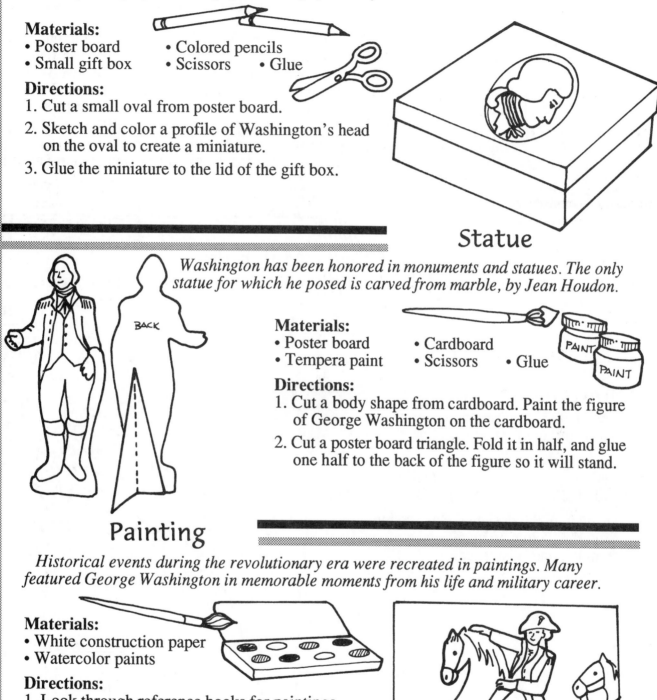

Washington has been honored in monuments and statues. The only statue for which he posed is carved from marble, by Jean Houdon.

Materials:
- Poster board
- Tempera paint
- Cardboard
- Scissors
- Glue

Directions:
1. Cut a body shape from cardboard. Paint the figure of George Washington on the cardboard.
2. Cut a poster board triangle. Fold it in half, and glue one half to the back of the figure so it will stand.

Painting

Historical events during the revolutionary era were recreated in paintings. Many featured George Washington in memorable moments from his life and military career.

Materials:
- White construction paper
- Watercolor paints

Directions:
1. Look through reference books for paintings featuring George Washington.
2. Use the paintings, plus information you know about the Revolutionary War, to paint a picture that features George Washington.

A National Flag

Historical Aid

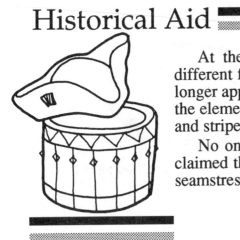

At the start of the Revolutionary War, Americans fought under many different flags. After the Declaration of Independence, the British flag was no longer appropriate. In 1777, the Continental Congress issued a resolve defining the elements to be incorporated into a national flag: red, white, and blue; stars and stripes. No specific design came about until several decades later.

No one knows who made the first flag. Congressman Francis Hopkinson claimed that he had designed it. Legend has it that Betsy Ross, a Philadelphia seamstress, made the first U.S. flag. Most historians do not support this claim.

Project

Design the "first" national flag.

Materials

- Red, white, and blue construction paper
- Large sheet white construction paper
- Scissors
- Glue

Directions

1. Imagine it is your job to design the first national flag of the United States.

2. Keeping the designated elements in mind (red, white, and blue; stars and stripes), cut and glue construction paper to create a flag.

3. Display all the designs. In a "session of Congress," vote on an official national flag from the ones displayed.